THE CH
FOR (

MW01008276

JESUS

REV. JUDE WINKLER, OFM Conv.

Imprimi Potest: Mark Curesky, OFM Conv., Minister Provincial of St. Anthony of Padua Province (USA)
Nihil Obstat: James T. O'Connor, S.T.D., Censor Librorum
Imprimatur: ✠ Patrick J. Sheridan, D.D., Vicar General, Archdiocese of New York

The Nihil Obstat and Imprimatur are official declarations that a book or pamphlet is free of doctrinal or moral error. No implication is contained therein that those who have granted the Nihil Obstat and Imprimatur agree with the contents, opinions or statements expressed.

THE CHURCH YEAR

I T seems as if we are always waiting for something. We are always looking at the calendar to see how much time is left until our birthday or Christmas or whatever day we can celebrate.

We have big days in the Church as well. In fact, the Church has a calendar filled with celebrations and festivals. We call this calendar the Church Year. It recalls and helps us celebrate the various stages of Christ's life, which are called mysteries.

Like any calendar, there is a day to mark the beginning of the new year. The Church Year does not begin on January 1, however, but rather on the First Sunday of Advent.

Advent is a period of about four weeks during which we prepare for the birth of Jesus, which we celebrate on Christmas Day (December 25). There are special prayers and acts of penance to make room in our hearts for Jesus. The priest wears purple vestments as a sign that this is a time of penance.

As Christmas draws near, preparations become more and more intense. The Third Sunday of Advent, in fact, is a Sunday of joy because the waiting is almost over. Then, from December 17, there are special readings and prayers to remind us that these are the last days in which we can prepare ourselves for the birth of Jesus.

CHRISTMAS DAY

FINALLY, after almost a month of preparations, Christmas day arrives.

Every year we celebrate Christmas on December 25, no matter which day of the week that is. Though this feast does not always fall on a Sunday, we give it all the honor and dignity of the greatest of holidays.

We are not really sure of the actual day on which Jesus was born. In the Gospels we hear that the shepherds were watching over their sheep by night when Jesus was born, something that they only do when the sheep are giving birth to lambs. This takes place in March or April of each year.

Then why do we celebrate Christmas on December 25? No one knew the exact day on which Jesus was born, so the early Christians decided to choose a day to celebrate their great event. They chose a day that was already a Roman pagan holiday, the feast of the birth of the Sun. That holiday was celebrated in the days just before December 25 because these are the shortest days of the year, but around that time the days start to get longer (as if the sun is reborn).

So from then on Christians have celebrated Christmas on December 25.

EPIPHANY

C HRISTMAS is such an important feast that it is impossible to celebrate it only for one day.

The days immediately following Christmas are part of one long celebration that we call the octave. For eight days, we say the prayers that have been written for Christmas Day, as if Christmas were really eight days long.

Then, on January 6, we celebrate one of the important events of the Christmas season. It is the feast of the Epiphany.

The Gospel of Matthew tells us that when Jesus was born, a star rose in the sky and announced his birth. A group of Magi, men who watched the night sky to read the messages of the stars, saw this star and traveled to Bethlehem to pay homage to this newborn king.

The Magi brought gifts for Jesus: gold, the gift one would give to a king; frankincense, the incense one would burn to give honor to God; and myrrh, an ointment used to prepare the dead for the burial, for it foretold the fact that Jesus would die for our sins.

In many countries, the Epiphany is almost as important as Christmas Day. People often follow the example of the Magi and exchange their presents on that day instead of Christmas Eve.

LENT

L ATE in the winter or early in the spring, we enter into another period of preparation. For forty days and nights, we celebrate Lent, a period of fasting and conversion as we prepare ourselves for Easter.

Lent is forty days long for it reminds us of the forty years that the Jews spent in the desert as they prepared to enter the promised land. It also reminds us of the forty days and nights that Jesus spent fasting and praying in the desert as He prepared for His public ministry.

Lent begins with Ash Wednesday. Ashes are placed on our forehead and we are told either, "Turn away from sin and be faithful to the Gospel," or "Remember, man, you are dust, and to dust you will return."

This first saying reminds us that during Lent we are to fast and do penance just as Jesus did. We give up our favorite foods as a sign of the fact that Jesus is more important to us than anything that we eat. We also reach out to those who need our love.

The second saying reminds us that we will not live forever. We cannot sit around and say that there is always time to do good tomorrow.

From Ash Wednesday until Easter, priests wear purple vestments to remind us that, like Advent, this is a season for doing penance.

9

10

HOLY THURSDAY AND GOOD FRIDAY

L ENT, our period of fasting and doing penance, ends on the Wednesday before Easter. Then, on Thursday and Friday, we commemorate the last events of Jesus' life on earth and the way in which He died.

On Thursday, the day we call Holy Thursday, we remember how Jesus called His disciples together to eat a special meal with Him the night before He died.

We call this meal the Last Supper. During that meal, Jesus took bread, broke it, and gave it to His disciples saying, "Take and eat, all of you, this is My Body which will be given up for you."

Then, at the end of the meal, He took a cup of wine, gave it to His disciples and said, "Take this, all of you, and drink from it. This is the cup of My Blood, the Blood of the new and everlasting Covenant which will be given up for you. Do this in memory of Me."

Most important feasts of the Church year are celebrated with a special Mass, but on Good Friday we do not celebrate a Mass at all. We gather together and read the story of how Jesus suffered and died for us. We then kiss the Cross, for it was through the Cross that Jesus freed us from our sins.

EASTER SUNDAY

SATURDAY, the day after Good Friday, is a day of great expectation. That evening we begin to celebrate the great feast of Easter when Jesus rose from the dead. When the sun has gone down, we gather in the darkness of our church and pray. The priest leads us outside of the church where he lights a fire and blesses it.

On that evening we bless the Paschal Candle, a large candle that we burn all throughout our Easter Season. The candle is carried in the church while the deacon sings that Jesus is the light of the world. We also bless the water used to baptize people into the family of Christ.

Often, in fact, this is the night in which we celebrate the Baptism of those who have been preparing to enter into the Church. We also take part in this Easter commitment, for we are all asked to renew our own baptismal promises. The newly baptized Christians are also confirmed with a special oil, the chrism, which our Bishop blessed during a special Mass on the morning of Holy Thursday.

While we have fasted all of Lent as we prepared for Easter, we now begin a period of rejoicing. We fill our churches with flowers and music. The "Alleluia" and the "Glory to God in the Highest" are sung again and again. We even eat Easter candy as a sign of joy because of Jesus' great victory over death.

13

14

ASCENSION THURSDAY

J UST as our preparation for Easter lasted for forty days and nights, so also our celebration of the Resurrection of Jesus lasts forty days and nights.

These forty days recall how Jesus appeared to His disciples after His Resurrection. Throughout the Easter Season, we read the accounts of His appearances and how He encouraged and taught His disciples, preparing them for their mission. All of this time, priests wear white vestments when they celebrate the Mass, for white is a sign of joy. And every time that we gather to pray, we sing "Alleluia" over and over again, for it is a call to rejoice and to praise the Lord.

Then, at the end of the forty days, we celebrate Ascension Thursday. This feast recalls the day when Jesus took His disciples to a hill just outside of Jerusalem. He blessed them and told them that they must now preach His message throughout the whole world. He was then taken up from their sight into the clouds, for He now sits at the right hand of the Father.

The disciples stood around for a while, confused. But an angel appeared to them and told them to return to Jerusalem and to pray for the coming of the Spirit.

PENTECOST

JESUS did not abandon us. He promised that He would send us the Holy Spirit to continue to teach and guide us.

The disciples returned to Jerusalem from that hillside on Ascension Thursday and they went into the Upper Room. They locked the doors of the place where they were staying for fear of the Jews. They prayed as they awaited the coming of the Spirit.

Then on the tenth day, the day of the Jewish feast of Pentecost, the disciples and Mary were praying when they heard a great wind. The Holy Spirit descended upon them in the form of tongues of fire. This Spirit filled them with courage and understanding.

Peter and the disciples opened up the doors to that place and they began to preach to the crowd that was gathered to see what was happening. They proclaimed that Jesus had died for them and had won forgiveness for their sins. But God had raised Jesus from the dead and the Father and the Son had now sent the Spirit as a fulfillment of their promise.

On Pentecost, we recall the gift of the Holy Spirit, which we received in our Baptism and Confirmation. The priest wears red to recall the tongues of fire that descended upon the disciples.

SUNDAY, THE LORD'S DAY

A LL of these holy days are reminders of God's great love for us, but these are not the only celebrations that we have. Every Sunday we celebrate the day on which Jesus rose from the dead.

In the Old Testament, the Jews were given the commandment that they were to keep holy the Lord's Day. For the Jews, that day was the Sabbath, the seventh day of the week, which we call Saturday. In this day, the Jewish people spend their Saturdays (from sunset on Friday until sunset on Saturday) praying and resting from their work.

After Jesus rose from the dead, His followers realized that Sunday, the first day of the week and the day on which Jesus rose from the dead, was now the day that Christians should keep holy. They gathered together and repeated the actions and words that Jesus had taught them at the Last Supper.

We have already seen that during Advent and Lent priests wear purple vestments, while on Christmas, Easter, and other great feasts they wear white. Red is the color worn on Pentecost. On most of the other Sundays of the year, priests wear green, for it is the color worn during what is called the Ordinary Time of the year.

MARY, MOTHER OF GOD

U P to this point, we have spoken of feasts that recall the Life, Death, and Resurrection of Jesus and the sending of the Holy Spirit. Each and every Sunday is a reminder of the day when Jesus rose from the dead.

But there are also feasts to recall the joy of those who listened to Jesus' call and followed Him with love. Greatest among the holy ones of God, His Saints, is Mary. She, among all people who ever lived, was the most loving of those who answered God's call.

On January 1, we celebrate a great feast of Mary's love. It is the feast of Mary, the Mother of God.

Mary was a young woman who was engaged to a man named Joseph in the village of Nazareth. One day Mary was greeted by an angel of the Lord named Gabriel who said, "Hail Mary, full of grace, the Lord is with you."

Mary was confused over the meaning of this saying, and the angel told her that she would become the Mother of a Son named Jesus. This would happen through the power of the Holy Spirit. Mary, with great generosity, responded, "Behold the servant of the Lord. Let it be done unto me according to your word."

THE ASSUMPTION

ON August 15, we celebrate another of the feasts that recall Mary and her life of service to the Word of God.

When Jesus was dying on the Cross, He spoke to His beloved disciple and to Mary. To the disciple He said, "Son, behold your Mother." To Mary He said, "Woman, behold your son." From that day on, the beloved disciple took Mary into his home and cared for her.

Then, on the day of Pentecost, Mary was praying together with the disciples when the Holy Spirit descended upon them. For the rest of Mary's life, she continued to give witness to the love that God had shown to her and to all of the followers of her Son.

When her life upon this earth was over, God gave her a special blessing. He did not let her body lie in a tomb, but rather raised her up into heaven body and soul.

We celebrate this event on the feast of the Assumption, on August 15. On that day, we speak of God's great love for Mary and her great love for God. But we also speak of how God loves us, too, and how, like Mary, He will raise all of us up on the last day into heaven, body and soul, to share in His life forever.

THE IMMACULATE CONCEPTION

THERE are many other feasts that honor Mary throughout the year. There is the feast of Mary, Queen of the Rosary; Mary, Our Lady of the Snows; Mary, Our Lady of Lourdes, and many others.

In addition to the feasts of January 1, Mary, the Mother of God; and August 15, the Assumption, there is one other feast dedicated to Mary that is a Holy Day of Obligation (a day on which all Catholics are to go to Mass). This other feast falls on December 8, and it is the feast of the Immaculate Conception.

When Adam and Eve sinned against God, they turned their backs upon the love of God. All of their children, everyone who was born after them, suffered from the effects of what they had done. We are all born into this world suffering from original sin.

Mary, however, is different. God so filled her with His love that from the moment of her conception, she did not suffer from original sin. This is what we celebrate on the feast of the Immaculate Conception. In order to prepare a holy one who would be the Mother of His Son, God protected Mary from the effects of sin from the earliest moment of her life.

THE SAINTS

THROUGHOUT the Church year, days are set aside to honor individual Saints. We honor the Saints who lived at the time of Christ—Joseph: March 19 and May 1; Peter and Paul: June 29; John: December 27; Mary Magdalene: July 22; Simon and Jude: October 28. We also honor Saints who lived throughout the ages—Benedict: July 11; Francis of Assisi: October 4; Clare of Assisi: August 11. There are even Saints who lived in our own days, such as Maximilian Kolbe: August 14.

The Church gives different levels of importance to those celebrations. For the very important Saints, we celebrate a *Solemnity*. For celebrations not quite as important, we celebrate *Feasts*. Finally, there are *Memorials*, which have even less importance.

Sometimes, even if the rest of the world is celebrating the feast of a particular Saint, we might celebrate that Saint with much greater honor. This happens when he or she is a Patron of our diocese or our parish or even our own personal Patron Saint.

There are different kinds of Saints whose feasts we celebrate. There are apostles, martyrs, and pastors (people who guided Christ's flock), virgins, etc. When we celebrate the feast of a martyr, the priest wears red to recall the blood of the martyr who died to give witness to God. On the other feasts, priests wear white as a sign of joy.

ALL SAINTS

T HE Church has chosen very many people who have lived throughout the ages and has proclaimed them as Saints. These are people who have given such good example in the way that they lived their lives that the Church holds them up to us as models of what it means to be a Christian in today's world.

In order to be certain that these people truly are Saints, the Church conducts a long investigation. It questions everyone who ever knew the person. It reads all of that person's writings. Then it prays for a sign from God. There must be at least two miracles obtained through that person's intercession before the Church will proclaim that person to be a Saint.

Yet there are millions and millions of other good people who are in heaven but whom the Church never officially proclaims as Saints. We celebrate the feast of these people on November 1: the feast of All Saints. This is the day that we celebrate God's goodness and His love toward all these people from all around the world and from all the ages. We also celebrate their generosity in responding lovingly to God's call.

The day after All Saints' Day, November 2, we celebrate All Souls' Day. This is the day on which we pray for all the souls in Purgatory, so that they might share in the joys of heaven.

A PRAYER FOR EVERY EVENT

IN addition to all of these celebrations, there are a number of different ceremonies and types of Masses that can be celebrated for various needs and various circumstances.

There are Masses for those who are getting married that speak of the blessings of married life. There are Masses to celebrate ordinations to the priesthood and diaconate and Masses for religious professions.

To share the sad moments of life, there are funeral Masses, during which we pray for the person who has died. We also pray for ourselves, that the Lord may console our hearts.

There is a special Mass that we use when we celebrate the Sacrament of Confirmation. There is a special feast to honor God's gift to us in the Sacrament of the Eucharist: the Feast of Corpus Christi, the Feast of the Body and Blood of Jesus.

We also have special prayers to give voice to particular needs. We have prayers for peace, prayers in time of drought, prayers for Christian unity and for many other needs. We have prayers to celebrate anniversaries of marriage, of ordination, and of religious profession. In other words, the Church has given us a way of voicing our every need, our every joy, our every sadness and our every fear, so that God can be part of every moment of our lives.

HOLY DAYS OF OBLIGATION

I N the United States, the following are Holy Days of Obligation (days on which all Catholics are obliged to attend Mass):

December 25:	**Christmas Day**
January 1:	**Solemnity of Mary, The Mother of God**
Ascension Thursday:	**The Thursday Forty Days After Easter**
August 15:	**The Assumption**
November 1:	**All Saints Day**
December 8:	**The Immaculate Conception**